Poems About Love
And
Other Dangerous
Things
2021 Edition

Michelle Torez

Copyright

About The Author

Michelle Torez is an established author, artist, motivational speaker and mental health campaigner. She has won various national and international writing awards. Due to Michelle enduring so much trauma and abuse in her life she has become an inspiration for many people, especially to those who have been let down and abused by the corrupt mental health system in the UK. Her poetry book 'Broken Doll' was ranked in the top 1,000 poetry books on Amazon UK due to its brutally raw depiction of abuse in the NHS mental health system.

Michelle was born in October 1994 in Hull, East Yorkshire, England. She was brought up by her loving father due to her mother having serious mental health problems. At the tender age of twelve following a mental breakdown, Michelle got locked away for a total of eight years in the inhumane mental health system. During her five year stay at Roycroft Clinic in Newcastle Upon Tyne, Michelle was sexually abused, physically beaten up, psychologically bullied and tortured and financially abused too, the money her father brought for her staff would steal. Michelle also witnessed boiling hot water being thrown at young children, children being starved, touched sexually and so much more.

Raising awareness of the lack of mental health care in the UK is Michelle's passion. Millions of people are being sent away from crisis teams and end up killing themselves, while some are getting trapped in hospitals for years and years being sexually and mentally tortured. Due to the disgusting lack of help in the UK, Michelle has lost many loved ones to suicide. She has stated many times that she will campaign for better mental health services for the rest of her life. Michelle currently lives in Leeds, England and is studying for a BA (Hons) in English Literature & Creative Writing with The Open University. She is working on her debut novel which is based closely on her own life story.

Other Titles By Michelle Torez

Poems About Love And Other Dangerous Things (2019 Edition)
Broken Doll-Poetry And Artwork From The Mental Hospital

My Novel Based On My Horrific Life Story
Is Coming Soon

I was just twelve years old. I hadn't even started my period, yet I was brutally thrown head first into the corrupt, cruel UK mental health system. I was subjected to sexual and mental abuse for years and then, when I was eventually released back into the community, was given very little support. This book details what exactly went on and how I actually survived.

Book coming soon!
Go to www.michelletorez.com for more info

Thank you for picking up this book. I hope that these poems inspire you. Writing is my life. It's my way of coping with the difficult times that life throws at you. It's my way of turning my experiences into a product for people to keep, hold in their hands and cherish.

I need to give out the message that anything is possible in this world, it really is. Please remember that, no matter how awful your situation may be right now, nothing stays the same forever.

Never give up
Michelle

I Know It's Hard To Believe Me

I know it's hard to believe me
when I say I've never felt like this before,
you've been force fed lies since you opened your eyes
but I knew I loved you when we met at your door.

I know you probably didn't believe me
when I promised to stick by you for life,
but I want nothing from you, just your happiness
to protect you I'd take a bullet, feel the knife.

I know it's hard to trust me
you've never experienced true love, I do understand,
that your idols were twisted and your childhood was stolen
so it's okay if you never hold my hand.

I know it's hard to believe me
but as the years go by, you will start to see,
that I mean what I say, I'm not letting you down
there is still hope left for humanity.

I Don't Bleed in Front Of You

Just because I don't bleed in front of you
doesn't mean that I never bleed,
the wounds that hurt the most
are the ones I don't let you see.

Don't be scared because you are my everything
I won't get too close, I know you don't need pressure,
but I've tried to protect you and will continue to
even if we are never together.

I need to thank you
you taught me that love isn't always
texting back quick,
passionate sex and handholding
I need to thank you
you taught me that love is giving your all
and not wanting a thing back
love is seeing way past her self-loathing.

So, just because I don't bleed in front of you
doesn't mean that I never bleed,
the wounds that hurt the most
are the ones I won't let you see.

Between A Rock And A Hard Place

She's stuck between a rock and a hard place
not wanting to hold it all in
but at the same time, not wanting to cry.

She's stuck between a rock and a hard place
not wanting to exist
but not exactly wanting to die.

If the dictionary had a photo beside the word 'hurt' it would have one of her. She would be laying on her sofa, fully clothed, wanting to sleep but in too much pain, her floor covered with unopened letters from the people that tried to get close to her but couldn't.

I Only Spoke To You

I only spoke to you
never did our hands touch, never did our lips meet
I imagine they would feel soft, tender
and taste of your favourite gum, minty and sweet.

I only spoke to you
and never did our words really mean anything,
apart from time passing, idle chatting
I only spoke to you about the world
never about the importance,
you with me,
and do you want to know why?
I knew you didn't care less really.

I only spoke to you
yet, I wanted so much more,
you and me snuggled under warm blankets
behind a reinforced, double locked door,
but, although I hate it, the thought that your now gone,
 your words help to remind me that
what feels so right can be
oh so wrong.

Personal Coping Again

I just need to masturbate in an empty, lifeless room,
while I think about everything that could've been
and all the ties that were cut too soon.

Uncomfortable

It's 7am and I've had my first coffee
outside the once pink faces are now pale,
I'm cold, c'mon pick up the phone to me darling
since when did your love for me go stale?

It's been six years but I'm not over us
they say time's a healer, but not when it's you,
I know you said it was just a bit of fun and to forget about it
 but we both know you loved me too.

Now my mind drifts across oceans
and my hands wander like succubus in the night,
I won't forget you, don't ask me to move on
I will find you and make this right.

Obsession

I'm living in a dark world
anything lit up is a danger to my self-esteem,
I tried to run away, I tried to hide
I tried to lick my deep wounds clean.

You're such a pain to my heart
it was only a matter of time before you caught me,
you screamed my name with such enthusiasm
I'm sorry to remind you but this isn't healthy.

I'm living in a dark world
and the truth is, I hated myself all along,
you sung at higher scales than me,
I wish I could have sung along

It Pours

It pours from me, the desperation
like water flows from a stream,
such urgency to fill up my heart's gaping hole
but at the same time, be kept clean.

With a friend, I will laugh and smile
suppressing my inner torment and distress,
but underneath the mask I wear so well
is a hurting woman surrounded by mess.

From afar you may see me as delicate
but please, try and not be so naïve,
every time I meet someone I'm starting
to plot, to control, to deceive.

Pain has changed me
I now push when the urge is to pull,
I now run when I really want to stay
my favourite dreams are nightmares
I never see in colour, always the grey.

You Are Going To Get Hurt

You are going to get hurt, it's a Human thing,
you'll feel cared for, cherished like a new born baby
then you'll be stabbed in the heart, tossed in a bin
that's what being Human is all about though my friend,
you are going to get hurt, be prepared for these things.

Most people don't care about you
but do care about taking all of your coins
so you can't afford to live,
these so called friends will force you
to worship your worst enemies
you will be drained, nothing left to give,
these so called friends will strip you of your dignity
and they most definitely will strip you of your pride,
then, when they need something again
they'll come knocking holding a card, flowers, maybe wine,
then, once again, you will accept it
even though you know they've not changed at all this time.

You are going to get hurt, it's a Human thing,
you'll feel cared for, cherished like a new born baby
then you'll be stabbed in the heart and tossed in a bin,
but that's what being Human is all about though my friend
you are going to get hurt, prepare for these things.

Karma

Awoken again by her voice, she loves to rob me of my sleep
my pillow gets soaked as I weep and I weep,
'you mustn't forget, what you give is what you get'
damn this room is bare now, filled only with regret.

I can see her outside the window
she doesn't look at me, she doesn't want to see,
the monster she created when she
turned away, walked away from me.

Sat in this cold room with even colder thoughts
that depression booklet over there won't save,
those condescending, patronizing sentences can't stop me
I've made up my mind, my bed is made.

Awoken again by her voice, she loves to rob me of my sleep
my pillow gets soaked as I weep and I weep,
'you mustn't forget, what you give is what you get'
damn this room is bare now, filled only with regret.

Narcotics

You dumped my love inside an urn
and tossed it in a closet,
next to the hearts of those you burned
since you became hooked on those narcotics.

I cracked your chest of secrets
only to see it contained nothing but dust
then you told me I did not love you
and that 'darling, its only lust'.

I just smiled and looked to the floor
I know you can't see past your pain,
but sadly I will never stop loving you
and it's unlikely you'll ever change.

Dark forces are at work. She is trying, oh so desperately,
to make angels
out of those that are obviously

demons.

If the devil says to walk
I'll go six steps further and run,
he has in his pocket the bullets
but in my hand I have the gun.

Vulnerable

In just under three hours she bore her soul to me
I was the witness as it all exploded out,
it was like an exorcism, so I just stayed calm
throughout her whispers, growls and shouts,
then, like confession, with closed eyes and pressed palms
she told me that she is an Atheist as religion only caused her
harm.

Pass Me The Gun

If you ask me, that woman you let linger around you
like a bad smell should be shot in the head,
not that I'm a violent person
or hold a deep rooted grudge or anything
it's just that you deserve so much better
and everyone but you can sense the evil
that seeps through her pours,
she is a selfish breed and does nothing for you
you deserve so much better
you deserve me
here, pass me the gun.

Bad Dog

I'm here sitting in the dark
a ruthless little animal all alone,
eating defenceless souls in a brew
picking flesh from every bone.

I'm like an angry, feral dog
always growling, always biting at your hands,
it may seem like I hate you
but you know I want to enter your land.

I may be a little strange
but you know I don't mean any harm,
sit next to me, talk to me for just a bit longer
 look past those warning alarms.

You're there sitting in the light
a so called angel, a figure of utter lies,
eating defenceless souls in a brew too
babe, it's about time we gave me and you a try.

I hope one day you will wake up and see that I'm right here,
I'm everything you need.

Thrill

This method of zero pleasure isn't working
I'm craving something more, I need a thrill,
 so the invisible wall you built to keep me out
will soon be knocked down, I need my fill.

Every Night Ends The Same

Every night ends the same
no moans, no orgasmic screams,
it's dull sex with no passion
a hot coffee with no sugar or cream.

It's like you have one foot in this love and one foot out
a part of me wants to drag you over
that thin line of uncertainty
be mine! be mine! be mine!
I desperately scream and shout.

A Forgotten Rose

A forgotten rose, dying of thirst
in the corner of such a beautiful room
hope for us dried up like dead petals,
we are now surrounded in nothing but gloom
I stopped wanting to nurture you, protect you,
without a single tear in my eye
you abused me and you broke me, so now go wither and die.

Heartbreak, rejection, heartache
I'm just not prepared to feel anymore,
I have no more parts of my soul in which you can break
there is nothing left of my heart to manipulate, smash or take
bend and break
I have nothing at stake.

The way you flaunt what you don't have is embarrassing
you crave the truth so listen carefully
as I state this one last time,
like an old photograph that's curled at the edges
darling you've had your time to shine.

A forgotten rose, dying of thirst
in the corner of such a beautiful room
hope for us dried up like dead petals,
we are now surrounded in nothing but gloom
I stopped wanting to nurture you, protect you,
without a single tear in my eye
you abused me and you broke me, so now go wither and die.

Cigarette Butts 2

Your healthy lungs will soon turn black
you can't always see the damage, not when it's inside,
the pain will bubble up to the surface one day though
then you'll cover your ruined body and hide.

You flick your cigarette ends on the floor
I've witnessed them end up in awkward positions,
forced in holes,
it reminds me of my daily routine about eight years ago
abused by creatures of only shell, no soul.

Your clean lungs will turn to dirty lungs
your full of life yet so close to death,
your habit reminds me of the things I hardly discuss
the things I can't change and can never forget.

I watch as your cig light burns bright
then I sigh as your cig light fades away,
although it's already happened and the damage is done
it's never too late to turn away.

No Interpreter 2

Visualize everything that makes you who you are
visualize everything that makes your life bearable
in this icy existence,
then throw it into the fire, those ever so seductive flames
you'll become me, a heretic reciting names.

This world is as foreign to me now as when I was born
no words I speak could ever make sense to you
no words you speak could ever make sense to me,
this grief has trapped me in one time, one place
and I'm not sure if I want to be set free.

So please just watch my tongue flick like a snake
so please just watch my mouth
as it twists and it turns
visualize everything you ever wanted
then sit back and watch it burn.

No Interpreter 3

You tell me I don't make any sense now when I talk
and it's suddenly changed,
the way I present myself, the way I walk,
you tell me you'd like an interpreter to understand my speech
but I'm sorry, there is no interpreter,
not for this language of grief.

He Let A Demon In

His once delicate voice
now so harsh and deep,
he let a demon in while dreaming
he couldn't fight it, far too weak,
he now talks about suicide and has fantasies about death
I just hope he says goodbye to me, before he takes his final
breath.

My heart aches and aches
he doesn't hug me like we're in 2005,
I don't mention it though, he's hurting
and I'm just grateful he's still alive,
when we touch he's freezing, he makes my body far too cold
what's inside of him isn't human, stolen, gone is his soul.

He doesn't have long left
the darkness has a tight grip on him
he's drained, he's empty, he's hurting
so he'd rather drown than try to swim
we talk less and less as the weeks go speeding by
I've faced the tragic fact that that soon he is going to die.

His once delicate voice
now so harsh and deep
he let a demon in while dreaming,
he couldn't fight it, far too weak,
he now talks about suicide and has fantasies about death
I just hope he says goodbye to me, before he takes his final
breath.

PLEASE DON'T LEAVE ME
PLEASE DON'T LEAVE ME
PLEASE DON'T LEAVE ME
PLEASE DON'T PLEASE DON'T LEAVE,
I NEED YOU, I NEED YOU, I NEED YOU

PLEASE DON'T LEAVE ME
PLEASE DON'T LEAVE ME
PLEASE DON'T PLEASE DON'T LEAVE ME
PLEASE DON'T LEAVE ME
PLEASE DON'T LEAVE ME
PLEASE DON'T LEAVE PLEASE DON'T
LEAVE ME
PLEASE DON'T LEAVE ME

PLEASE DON'T LEAVE ME
PLEASE DON'T LEAVE ME
PLEASE DON'T LEAVE ME

PLEASE I BEG YOU
PLEASE I BEG YOU

PLEASE I BEG YOU

PLEASE I BEG YOU

Please don't kill yourself.

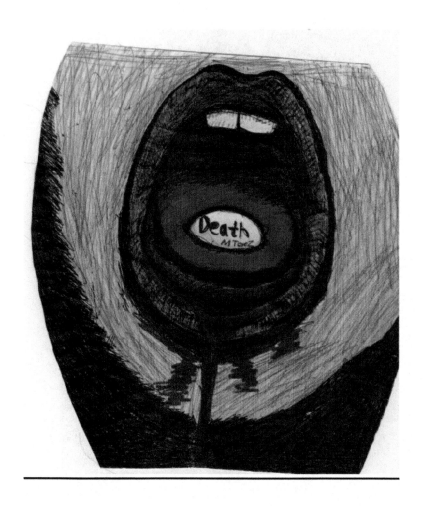

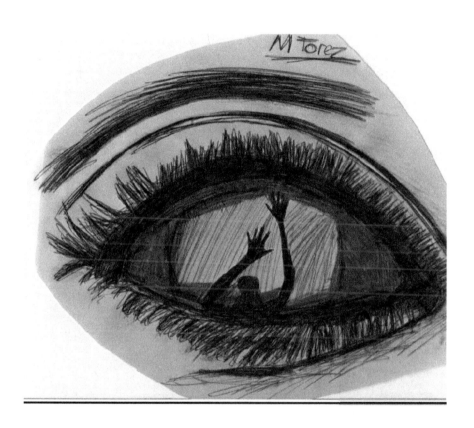

Very Sad Poem

Will you be alive tomorrow
will you be alive next week?
please open your mouth and tell me with sincerity
that death is no longer what you seek.

But, with a sigh I hold my tongue
some things will always be out of my hands,
'okay I love you' I say, before putting down the phone
his pain I understand.

It Was The Pieces That Couldn't Fit

I saw her in such beautiful full colour
when she could barely even see me in grey,
I pretended the ink on the love letters were dry
before she had finished what she truly had to say.

I chased her out of habit
it was the inner torment, the flirting with pain,
it was the lack of intimacy that kept me hungry for more
it was the pieces that couldn't fit that I framed.

Loneliness is a powerful force that always lingers
a dark entity disturbing my sleep,
I dreamt we were a couple and we could be happy
lying to myself is my coping technique.

I saw her in such beautiful full colour
when she could barely even see me in grey,
I pretended the ink on the love letters were dry
before she had finished what she truly had to say.

Now it's time to lock that door
now it's time to end the game,
now it's time to sit alone in a room
without the need to recite a name.

I chased her out of habit
it was the inner torment, it was the flirting with pain,
it was the lack of intimacy that left me hungry for more
it was the pieces that couldn't fit that I framed.

Dairy Entry 17

Last night, whilst holding her, I told her that she means everything to me. I think it scared her a little bit, poor woman. It's painfully obvious that she's afraid of genuine people, all she's familiar with is people with dark motives, soulless shells of people that want to take and take and take until there's nothing left then run. Well I'm proud to say that I'm not one of those people and I want to stick by this girl for the rest of my life, whether we end up together or not. I think, deep down, she knows all of this and it petrifies her. I completely understand though, she's been force fed lies since she opened her eyes, abused, let down then gobbled up and shat out. She has had a definite need for a wall of defence, so I don't blame her for not letting me past it. She thinks that she's completely broken, loveless, but I know that she's not, she's still got so much fight left in her to go on to achieve such incredible things. Despite everything she's seen, despite everything she's had to endure, there's still so much warmth left in her soul, there's still so much love in her heart that she wants to show, but she's just too scared, just in case she's used and thrown away again like a dirty dishcloth. It's been drilled into her subconscious to wear a safety mask of cold, insensitive, to push people away first so they can't do it to her. I can relate, I used to wear a similar mask myself, but my face outgrew it so one day I had to throw it away and set myself free. I hope one day she takes off her mask.

Birmingham New Street, 8pm

A woman approached me as I stood sipping my coffee outside of
Birmingham New Street train station and asked me if I needed
any;
'Spice, crack, whizz, blow
speed, coke, weed before it goes,
speedballs, acid, aerosols, shrooms,
lsd, poppers those are free for first use
even stronger poppers, angel dust or ecstasy
and I'll sell you some for cheap if you
promise to buy back from me.'

 I smiled, said no thank you and confessed that
 all I really   needed was a nice, warm hug.
'You must be on something already' she replied.

The Usual

The usual, we met online on a dating site
tanned skin, dark hair, my type,
we had chemistry, a real connection I kept telling myself
because we spent so many hours together on skype.

Two months later I asked her to be my girlfriend
after a two hour animalistic shag,
I'd like to say 'we made love' but of course we didn't
 it was just a fuck from behind with a gag.

'Yes, let's be together'
was celebrated with cocaine lines, lipstick stains,
I was naïve to think this was anything more than
two lonely girls trying to mask the pain.

The following Thursday she stayed once more
business as usual, drugs, sex and beer,
we were just damaged kids craving happiness endorphins
to suppress the fear of the inevitable looming near

I woke up two days later to find she'd gone
she'd blocked me on Facebook, Twitter, on phone,
so I rang her from a different number
only to be told 'I hate you, leave me alone.'

This hurt me but it didn't at all shock me
I knew this was going to happen, so didn't grieve,
damaged people sometimes only see what they want to
it's far easier to live in a world of make believe.

Superficial, barely scratching the surface is much safer
than exposing deep, open wounds to damaged souls,
we can satisfy our needs for just the right amount of time
before we both need to return to our dark holes.

The usual, we met online on a dating site
tanned skin, dark hair, my type,
within two months we were together
within three she was gone from my life.

Escort

I invite her in, she strains a smile
for an hour I'll pretend sex is all I need,
I unhook her bra as she looks at her watch
fifty minutes then she can leave.

I kiss her with a passionless guilt
I chill her with my cold embrace,
when we fuck I think of someone else
so I can't even look at her face.

I tell her to stop when I've cum
she doesn't get to, this is about me,
she's done her job and I've done mine
distraction from the pain of being empty.

She opens the door to the black
'thanks'
door shuts, loud thud,
she slips quickly into the darkness and so do I
fantasies of suicide, a thirst for blood.

Ho

I used to think that I could numb my pain
by having mindless, risky sex
only a few words should be spoken,
because the deeper the connection the deeper it cuts
I don't want any love urges re awoken.

Thirty used condoms later I'm sat wide awake
'bisexual visibility day' flashes up on my phone,
I sigh and swipe it away
it's good to have options to escape being alone,
but sometimes exploring too many
becomes like too many chefs for a stew
it spoils what was once beautiful
I feel worn out, alone, used
a slut, whore, ho
and any other word similar to that
I found that having a bed strapped to my back
didn't numb a thing
but now there isn't any going back.

Thirst

All windows are covered
all doors are locked tight,
to prevent my hungry demon
prowling around after midnight.

I don't want commitment
my clocks are always frozen in time,
blood quenches my thirst, sex gives me fuel
is your clock ticking? if so, please be mine.

I've Been At It Again

I've been at it again
faking smiles, making pacts for power,
I've spoken to escorts, drug dealers, gangsters, the whole lot
answering calls and texts at every hour.

It's just that I need to be in control of something
you're not daft, you know how it goes,
I sleep with the devil just to feel something
and I sleep with his wife to distract from my woes.

The darkness seduces me
like bees stick to honey, worms stick to soil,
I've been at it again faking smiles, making pacts for power
but it's my life, my body to spoil.

Opposites

Find me a victim, someone desperate to be loved,
I'll then erode their hope in humanity
pluck feathers, one by one, from a dove.

Find me a martyr, an outcast preparing to die,
I'll restore their hope in humanity
I'll tell them there are no eyes in the sky.

Dairy Entry 21

This woman has helped me to realise that I've never truly loved anyone before. In the past it was all about good times, sex and 'text me back quick', sure I cared for them but nothing like this. This feels different. Sometimes we hardly talk but that's okay, she's got her own issues and she owes me nothing. If, one day, the fear of being loved completely consumed her and she cut me out of her chaotic life I'd still love her with every part of my soul and I can say that with certainty. This is the real deal and I've never once questioned it. I loved her ever since I met her that afternoon. Her curly black hair shone bright under the evening sun as she stood wearing all black and a nervous smile at the door. My first thought was 'damn, she's the one' but I'll never tell her that, there's only so much loveydovey a hurt person can comprehend. I think back and laugh out loud about how I tried so hard to 'play it cool' but was more bloody nervous than a child on the first day of secondary school. I was astounded by her beauty and tried so hard not to stare at her big, full lips covered in dark lipstick that I had the pounding desire to kiss and kiss until every last bit of it was on my face. I found her dark eyes ever so arousing too so I tried my best to avoid eye contact as well, in fact everything about her oozed sexiness so I just kept my eyes on the walls or the floor, safe bet. I remember how awkward my attempt at kissing for the first time was and I cringe, my kissing skills aren't as good as hers but I'm not normally that bad wow. I miss her already but don't want to tell her, I don't want to make her feel any pressure, she's got enough on her plate. I just hope that I get to see her again. I love her.

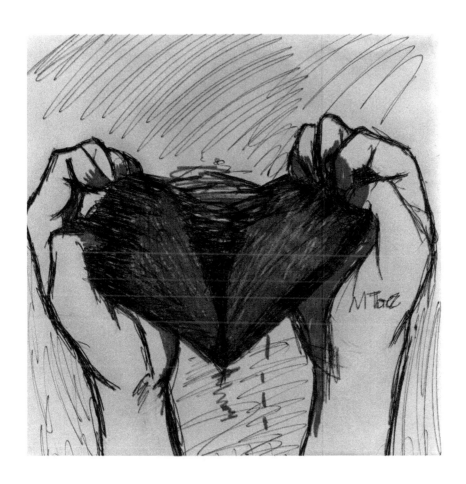

I didn't choose to fall in love with you
and you didn't choose to
feel love
le
s
s

Printed in Great Britain
by Amazon

40120052R00046